D0387044

If My Dogs
Were a Pair of
Middle-Aged Men

Other books by The Oatmeal

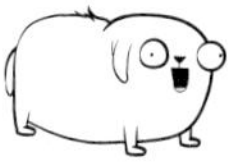

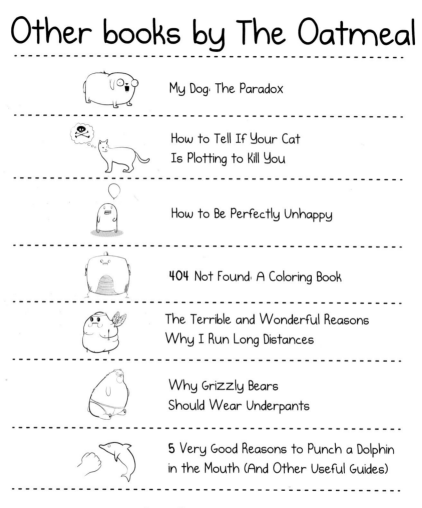

My Dog: The Paradox

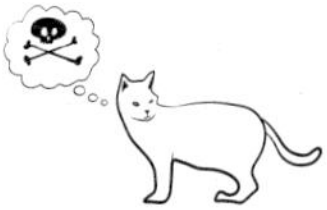

How to Tell If Your Cat
Is Plotting to Kill You

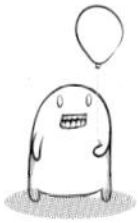

How to Be Perfectly Unhappy

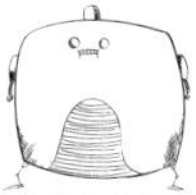

404 Not Found: A Coloring Book

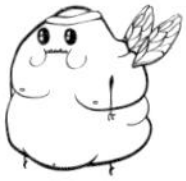

The Terrible and Wonderful Reasons
Why I Run Long Distances

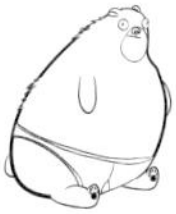

Why Grizzly Bears
Should Wear Underpants

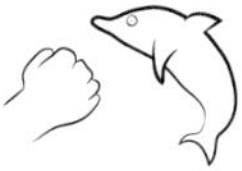

5 Very Good Reasons to Punch a Dolphin
in the Mouth (And Other Useful Guides)

www.TheOatmeal.com

If My Dogs
Were a Pair of
Middle-Aged Men

The Oatmeal

Andrews McMeel
PUBLISHING®

If My Dogs Were a Pair of Middle-Aged Men
copyright © 2017 by Oatmeal, LLC. All rights reserved.
Printed in China. No part of this book may be used or reproduced
in any manner whatsoever without written permission
except in the case of reprints in the context of reviews.

Andrews McMeel Publishing
a division of Andrews McMeel Universal
1130 Walnut Street, Kansas City, Missouri 64106

www.andrewsmcmeel.com

17 18 19 20 21 SDB 10 9 8 7 6 5 4 3 2 1

ISBN: 978-1-4494-3352-9

Editor: Patty Rice
Designer/Art Director: Diane Marsh
Production Editor: Erika Kuster
Production Manager: Tamara Haus

ATTENTION: SCHOOLS AND BUSINESSES
Andrews McMeel books are available at quantity discounts with
bulk purchase for educational, business, or sales promotional use.
For information, please e-mail the Andrews McMeel Publishing
Special Sales Department: specialsales@amuniversal.com.

This book is dedicated to my two idiot dogs, without whom I would probably be exactly where I am now, if not further.

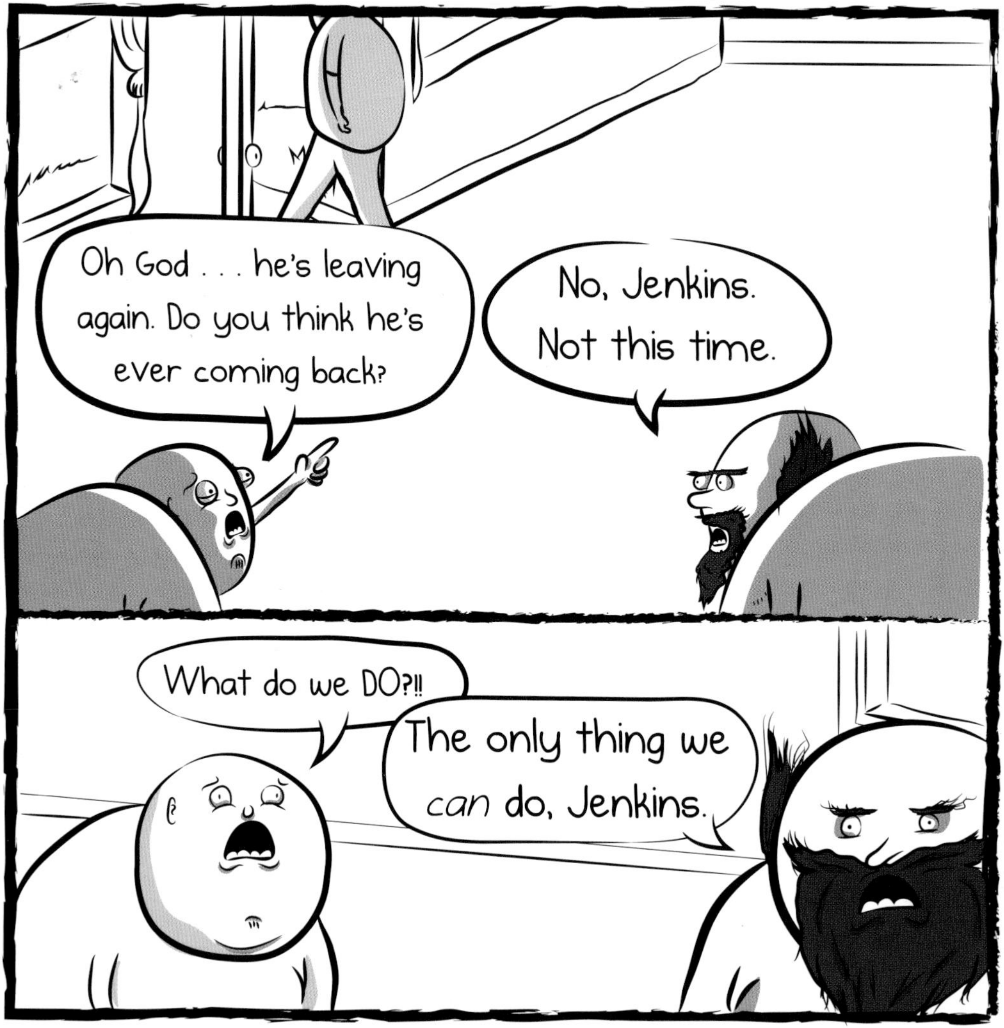
Oh God . . . he's leaving again. Do you think he's ever coming back?
No, Jenkins. Not this time.
What do we DO?!!
The only thing we *can* do, Jenkins.

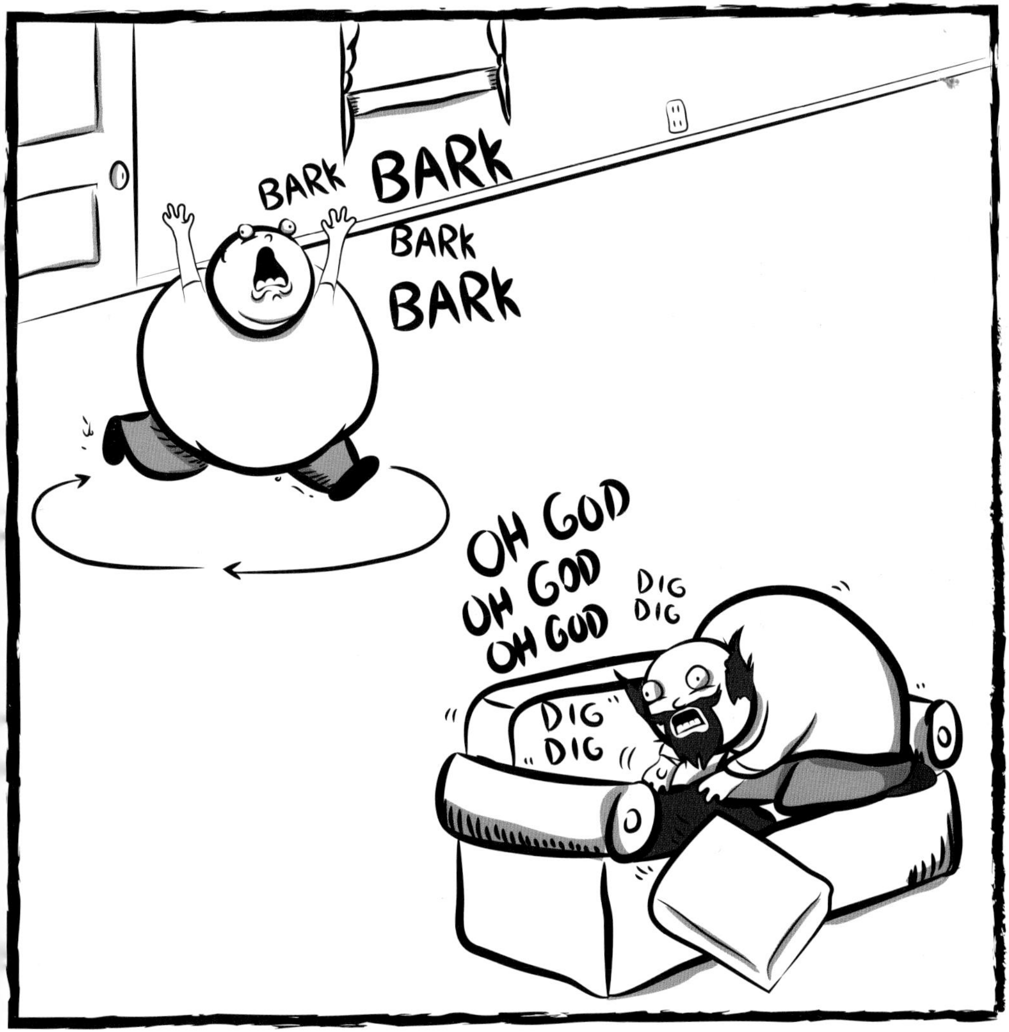
BARK BARK
BARK
BARK
OH GOD
OH GOD
OH GOD
DIG
DIG
DIG
DIG

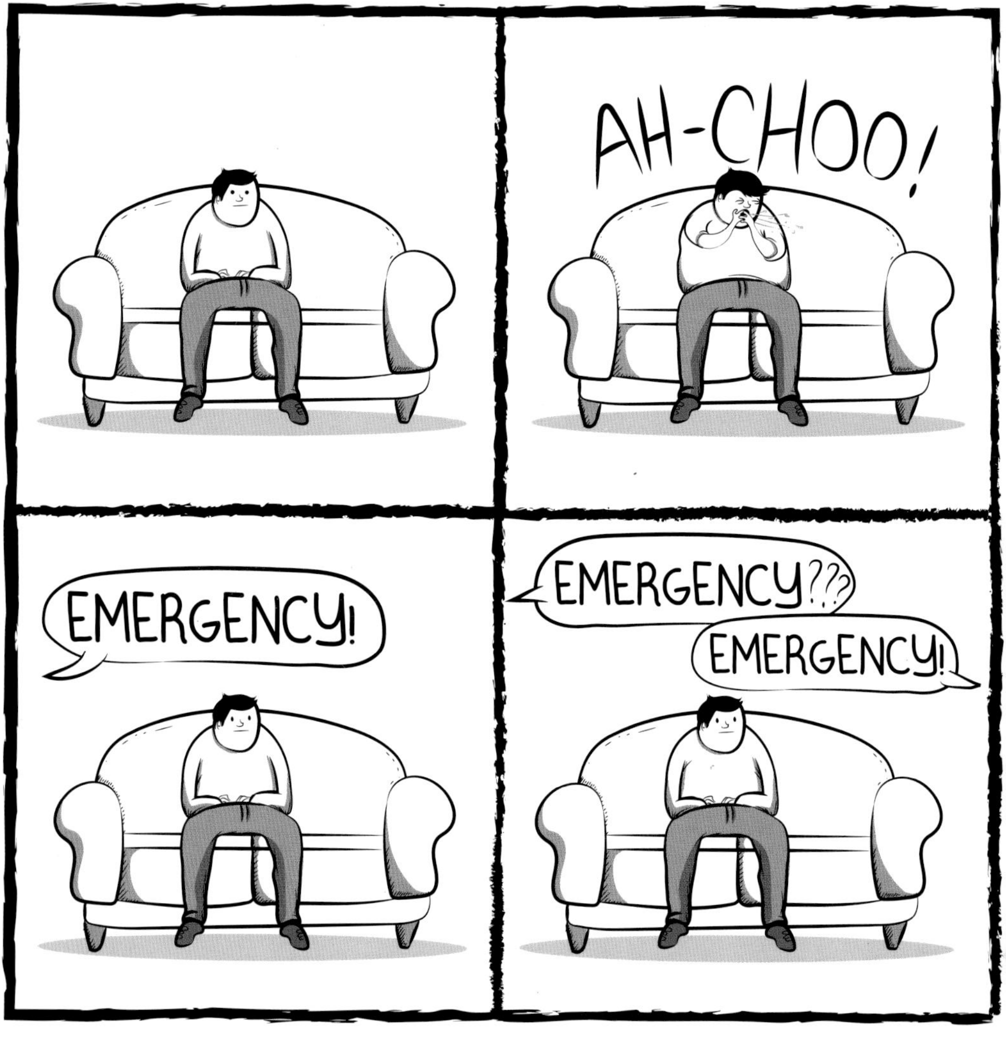
AH-CHOO!
EMERGENCY!
EMERGENCY???
EMERGENCY!

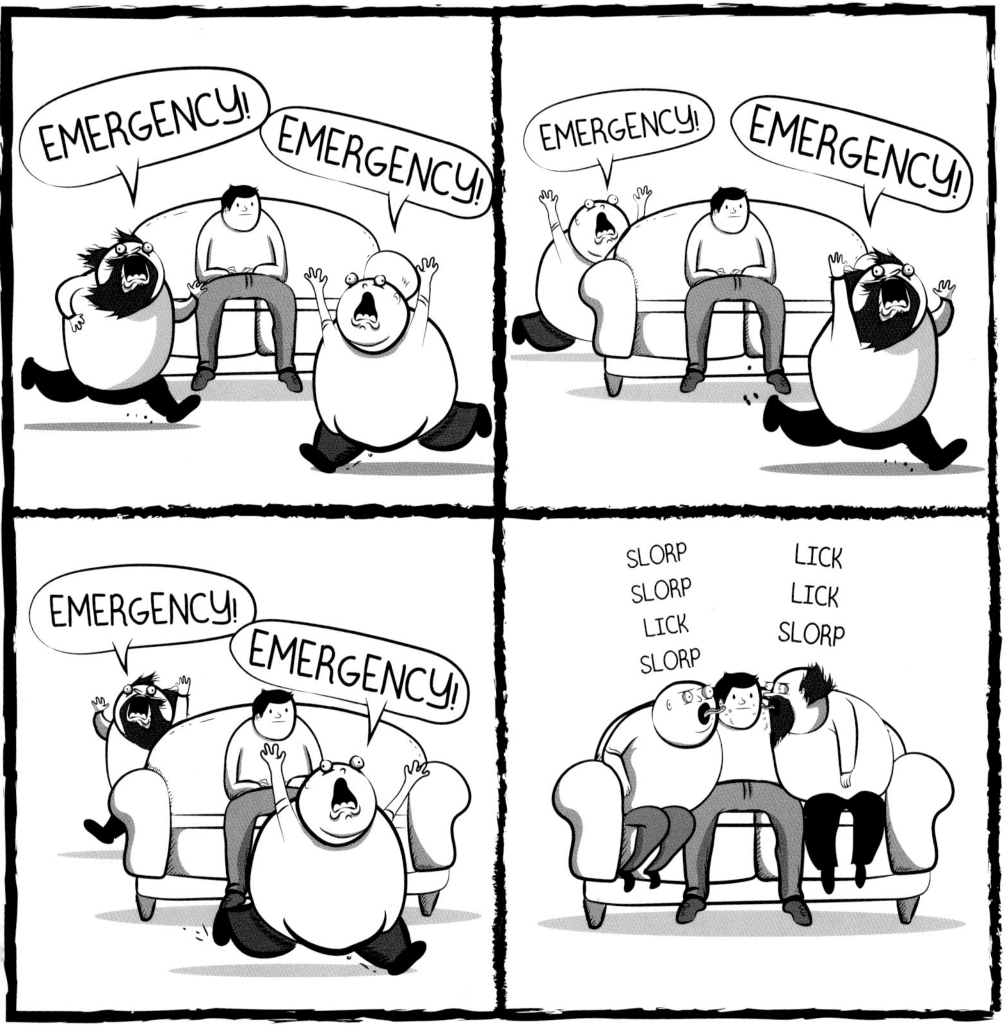
EMERGENCY!
EMERGENCY!
EMERGENCY!
EMERGENCY!
EMERGENCY!
EMERGENCY!
SLORP
SLORP
LICK
SLORP
LICK
LICK
SLORP

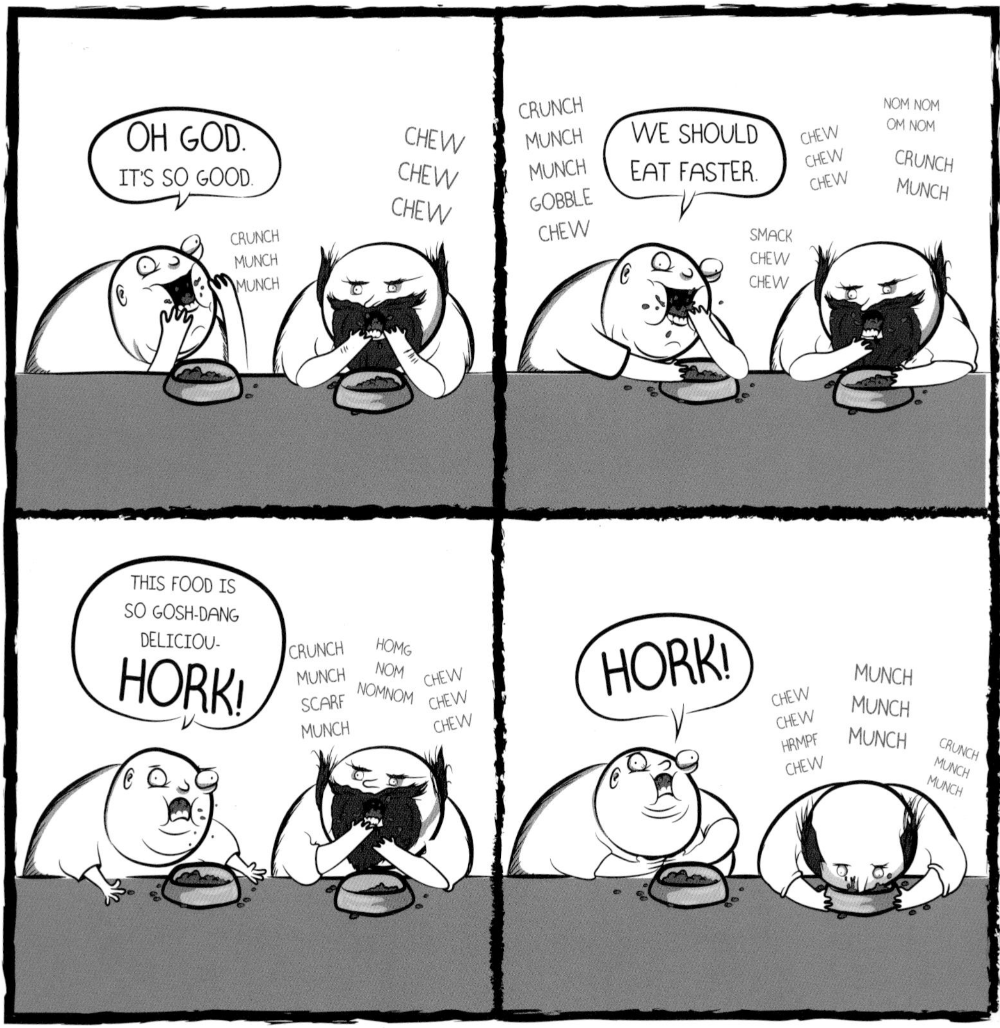
OH GOD.
IT'S SO GOOD.
CRUNCH MUNCH MUNCH
CHEW CHEW CHEW
CRUNCH MUNCH MUNCH GOBBLE CHEW
WE SHOULD EAT FASTER.
SMACK CHEW CHEW
CHEW CHEW CHEW
NOM NOM OM NOM
CRUNCH MUNCH
THIS FOOD IS SO GOSH-DANG DELICIOU-
HORK!
CRUNCH MUNCH SCARF MUNCH
HOMG NOM NOMNOM
CHEW CHEW CHEW
HORK!
CHEW CHEW HRMPF CHEW
MUNCH MUNCH MUNCH
CRUNCH MUNCH MUNCH

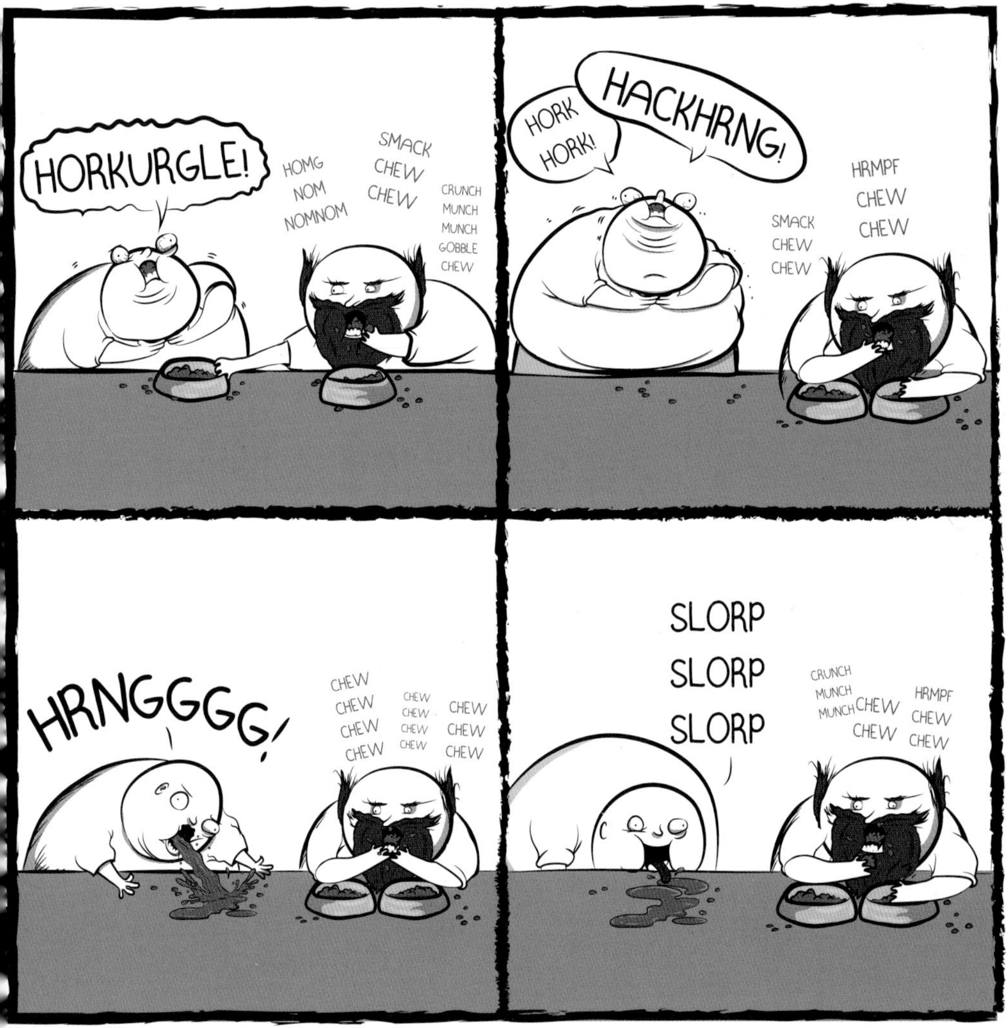
HORKURGLE!
HOMG NOM NOMNOM
SMACK CHEW CHEW
CRUNCH MUNCH MUNCH GOBBLE CHEW
HORK HORK!
HACKHRNG!
SMACK CHEW CHEW
HRMPF CHEW CHEW
HRNGGGG!
CHEW CHEW CHEW CHEW
CHEW CHEW CHEW CHEW
CHEW CHEW CHEW
SLORP SLORP SLORP
CRUNCH MUNCH MUNCH
CHEW CHEW
HRMPF CHEW CHEW

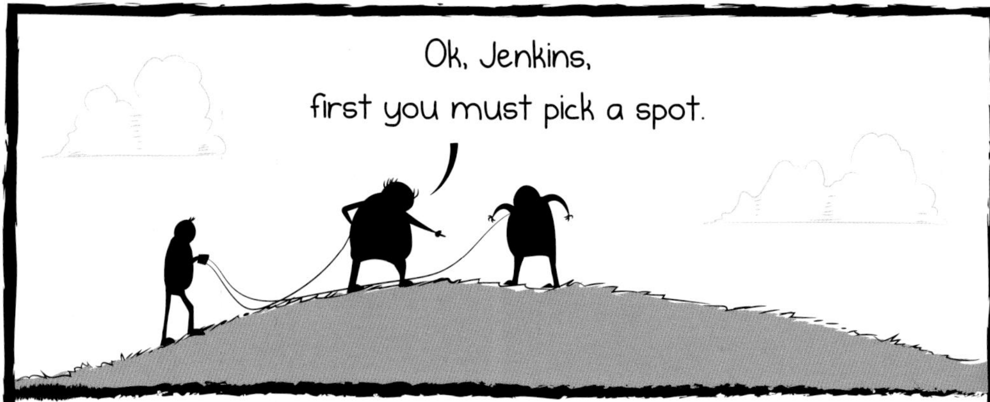
Ok, Jenkins,
first you must pick a spot.

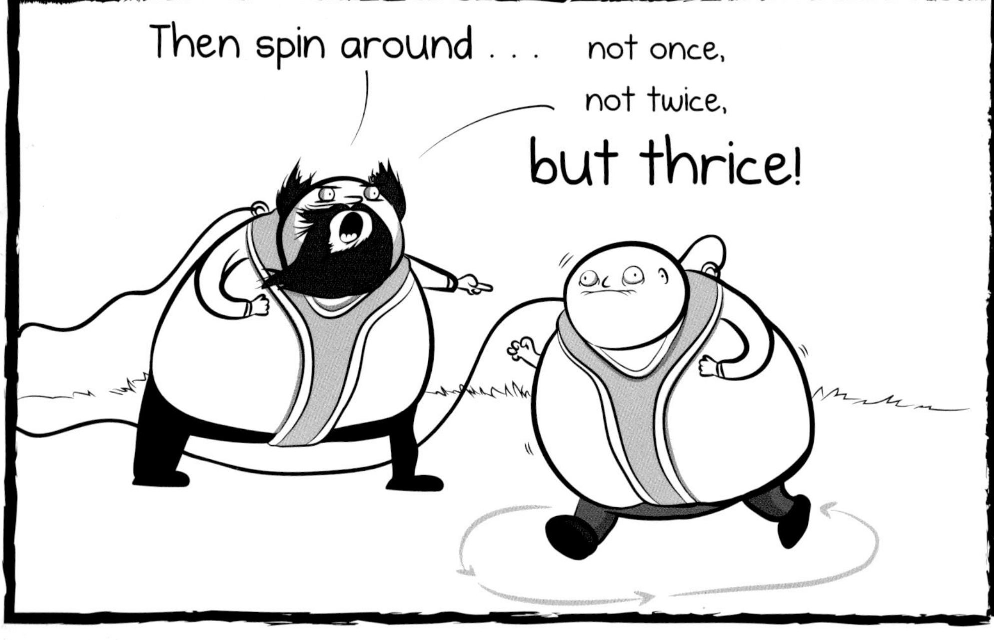
Then spin around . . .
not once,
not twice,
but thrice!

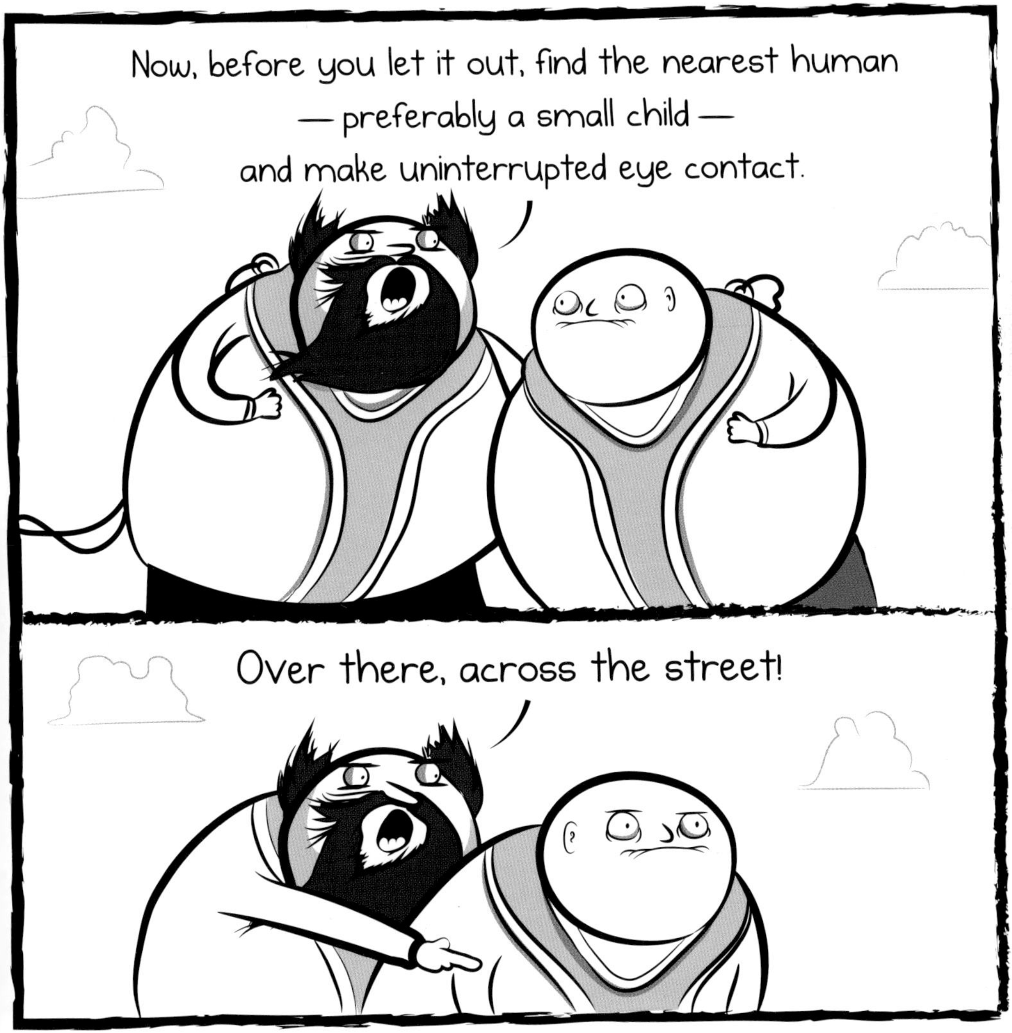
Now, before you let it out, find the nearest human
— preferably a small child —
and make uninterrupted eye contact.
Over there, across the street!

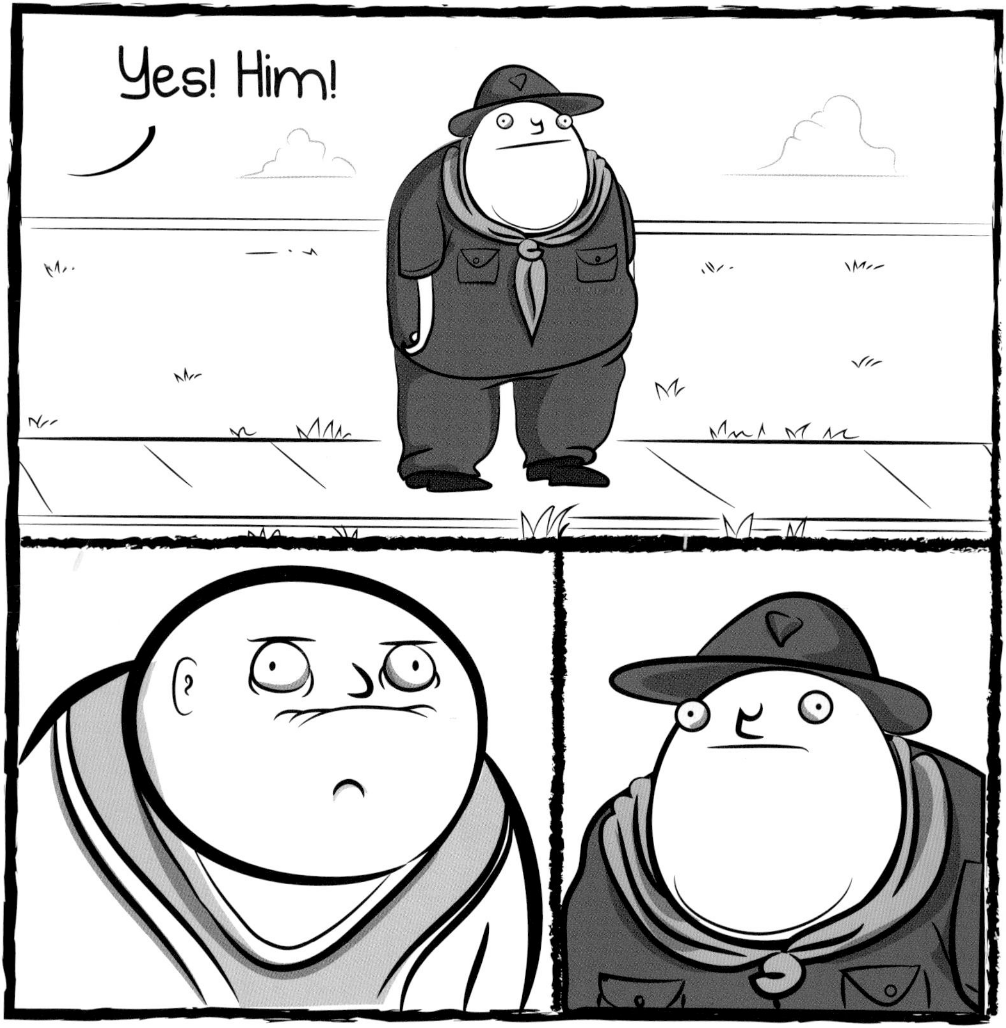
Yes! Him!

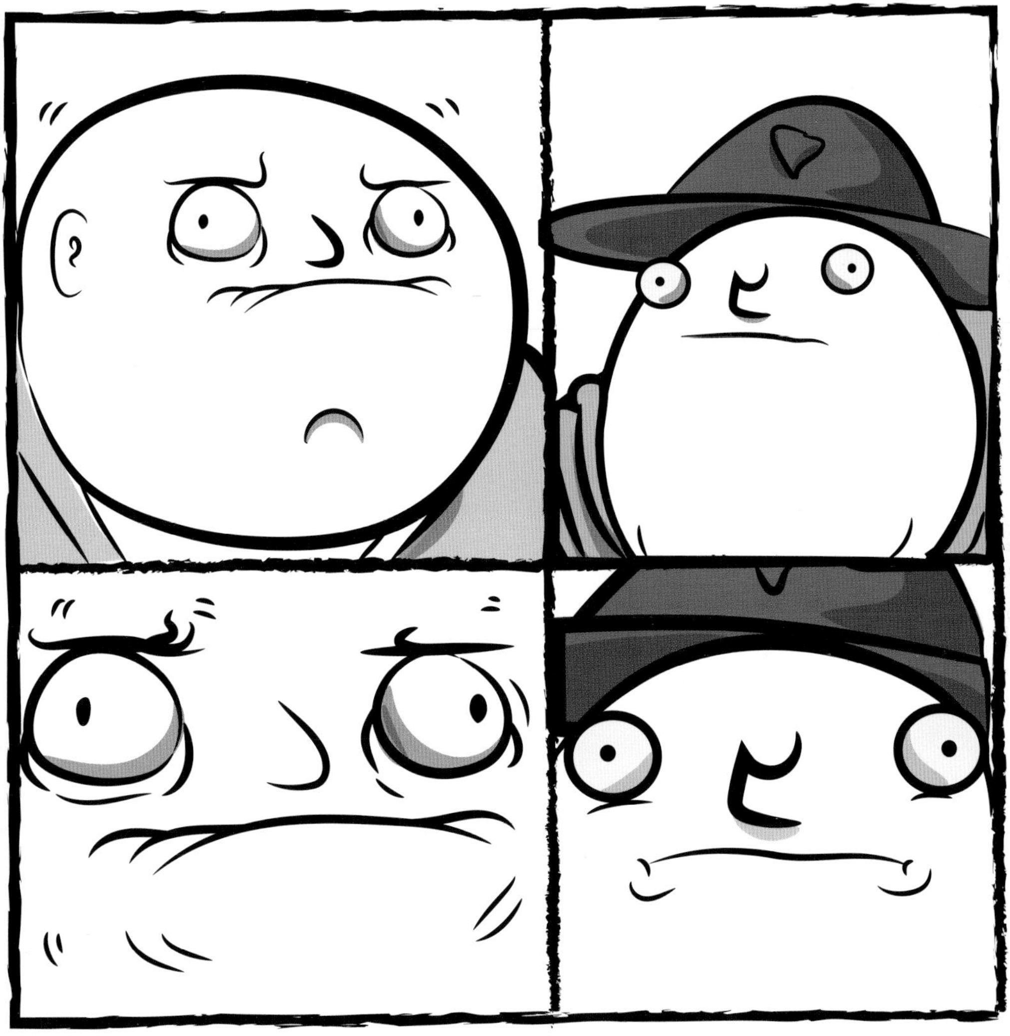

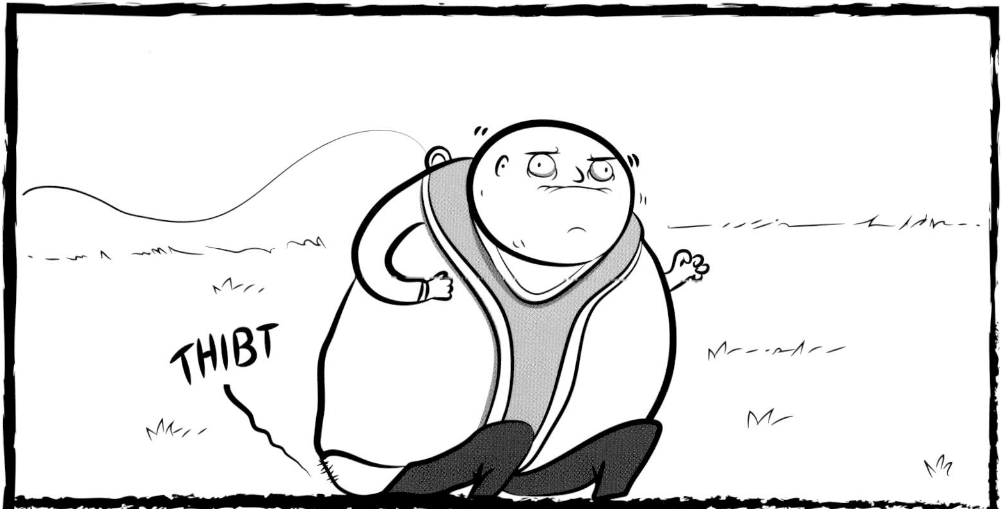
THIBT

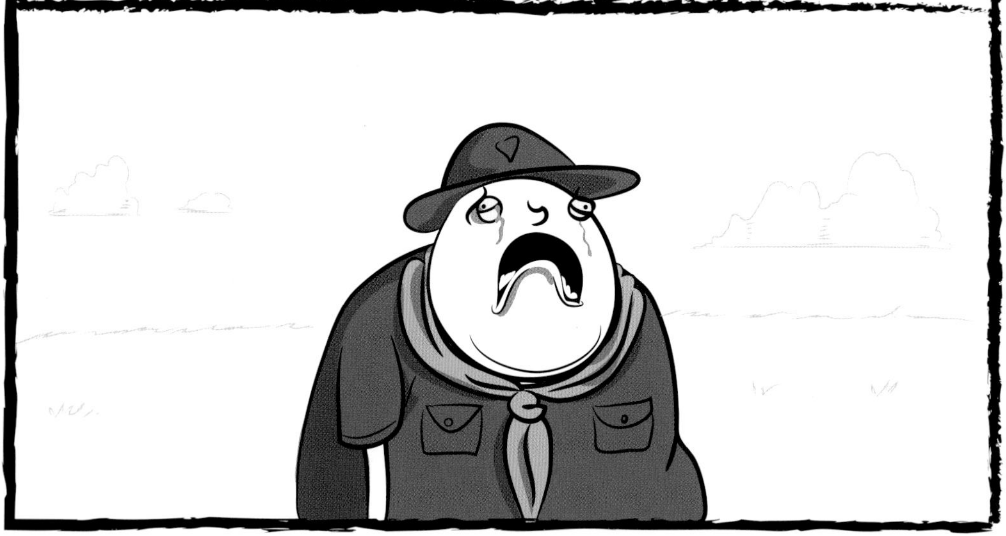

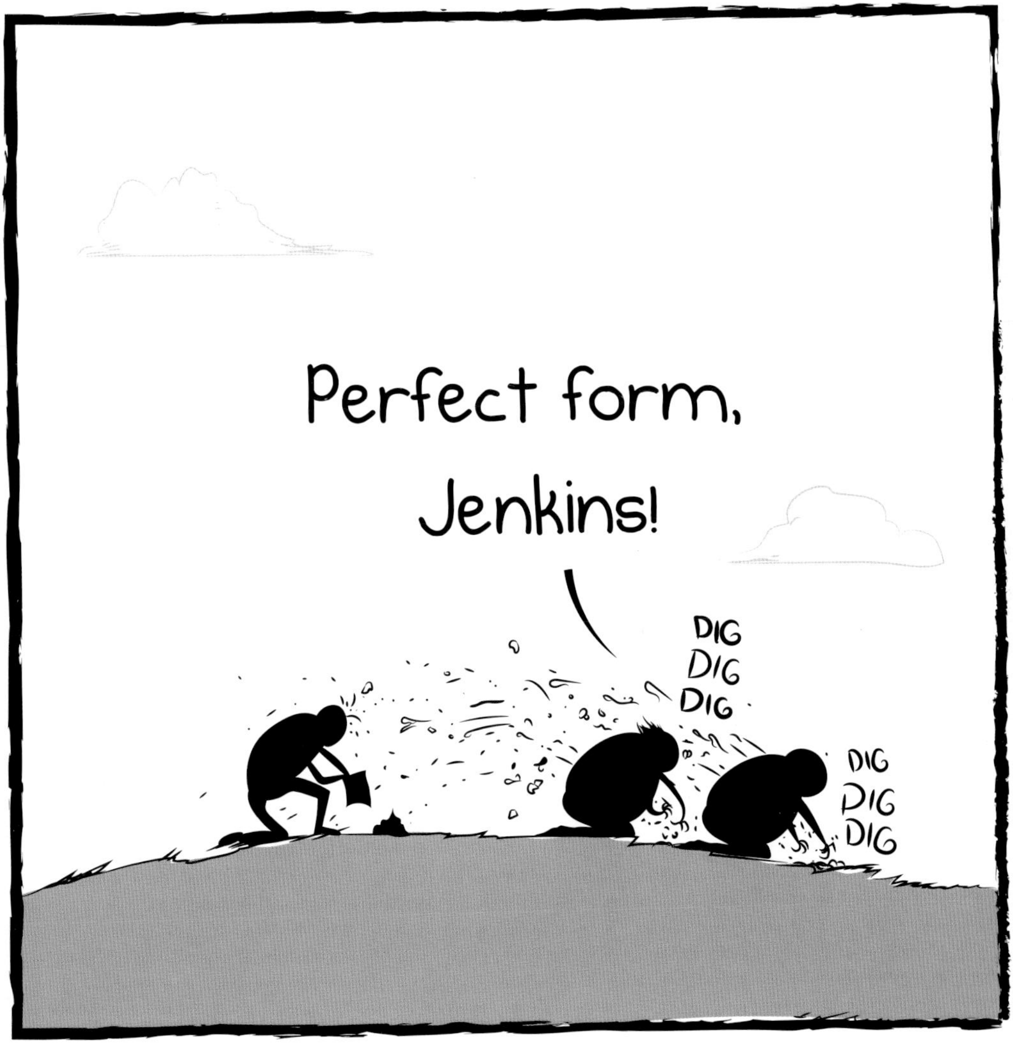
Perfect form, Jenkins!
DIG
DIG
DIG
DIG
DIG
DIG

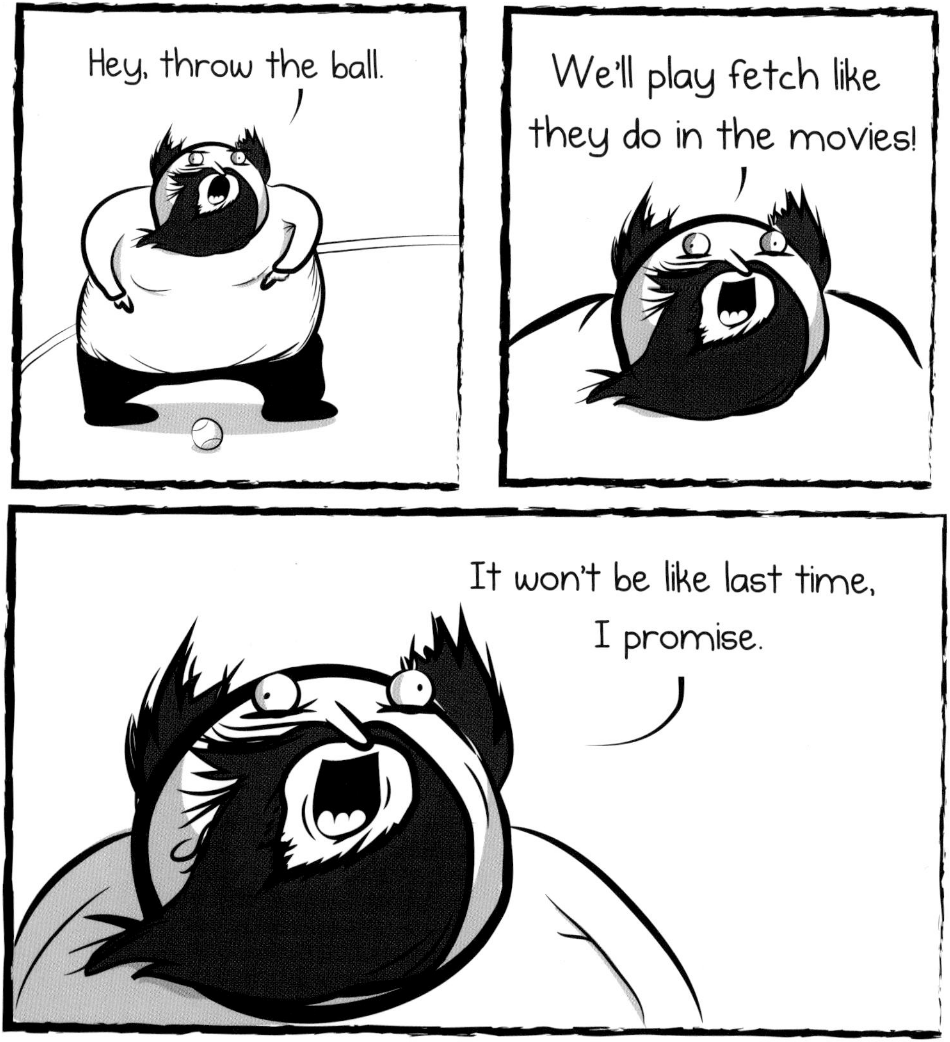
Hey, throw the ball.
We'll play fetch like they do in the movies!
It won't be like last time, I promise.

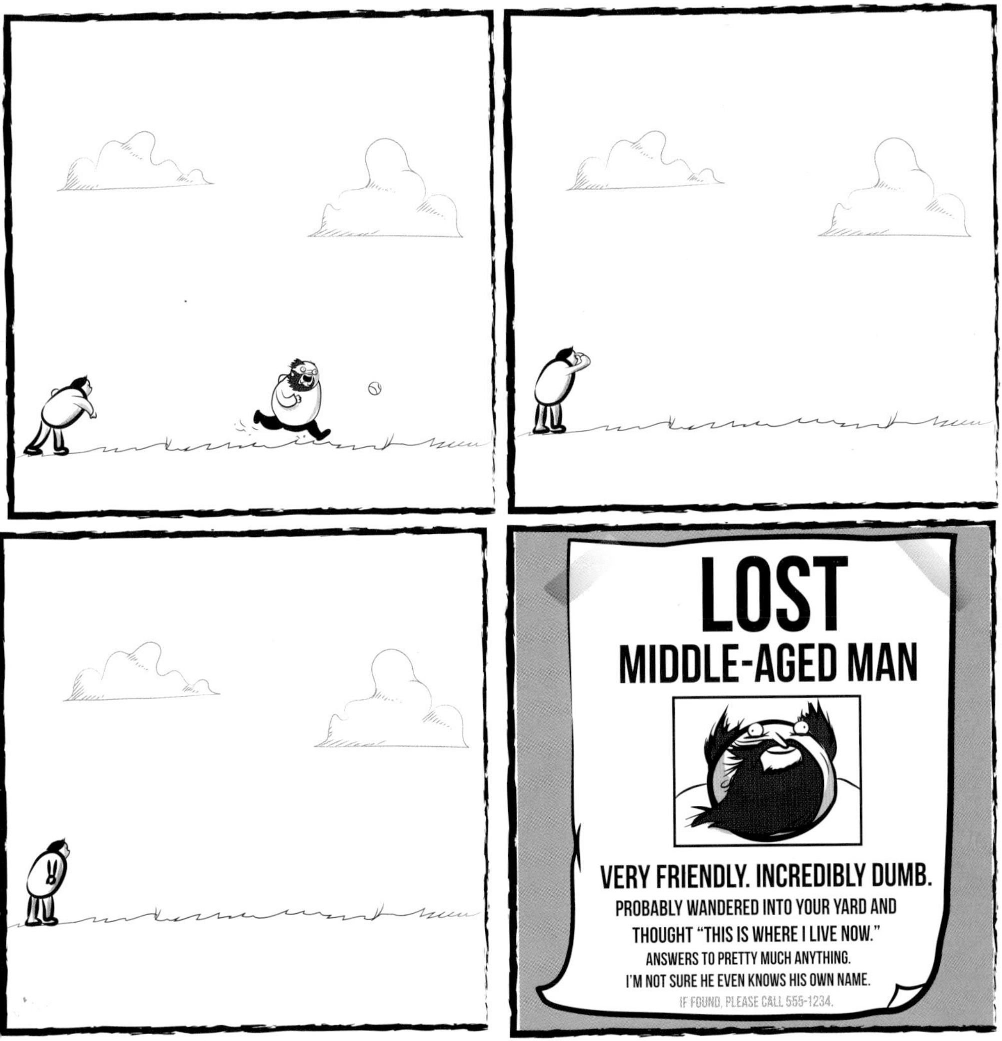
LOST
MIDDLE-AGED MAN
VERY FRIENDLY. INCREDIBLY DUMB.
PROBABLY WANDERED INTO YOUR YARD AND THOUGHT "THIS IS WHERE I LIVE NOW."
ANSWERS TO PRETTY MUCH ANYTHING.
I'M NOT SURE HE EVEN KNOWS HIS OWN NAME.
IF FOUND, PLEASE CALL 555-1234.

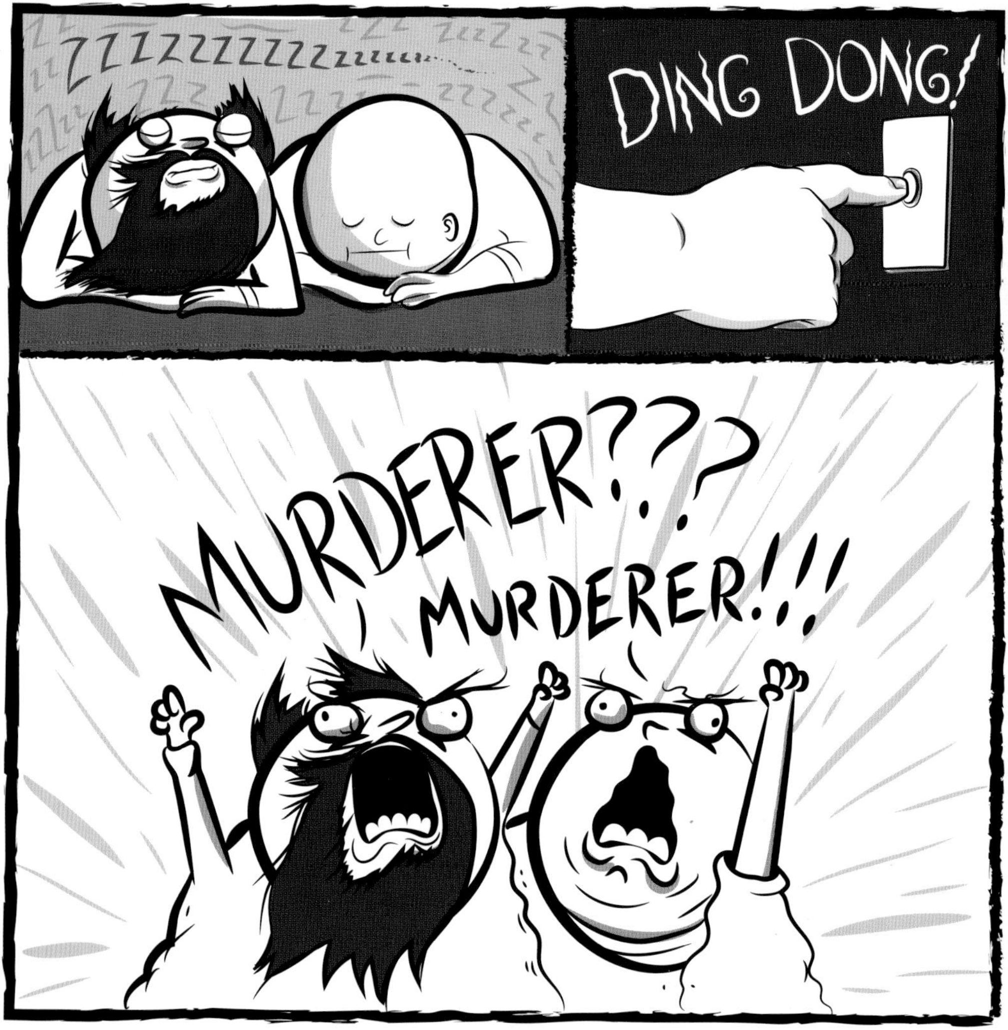
ZZZZZZZZZZZZZzzzzzz
DING DONG!
MURDERER???
MURDERER!!!

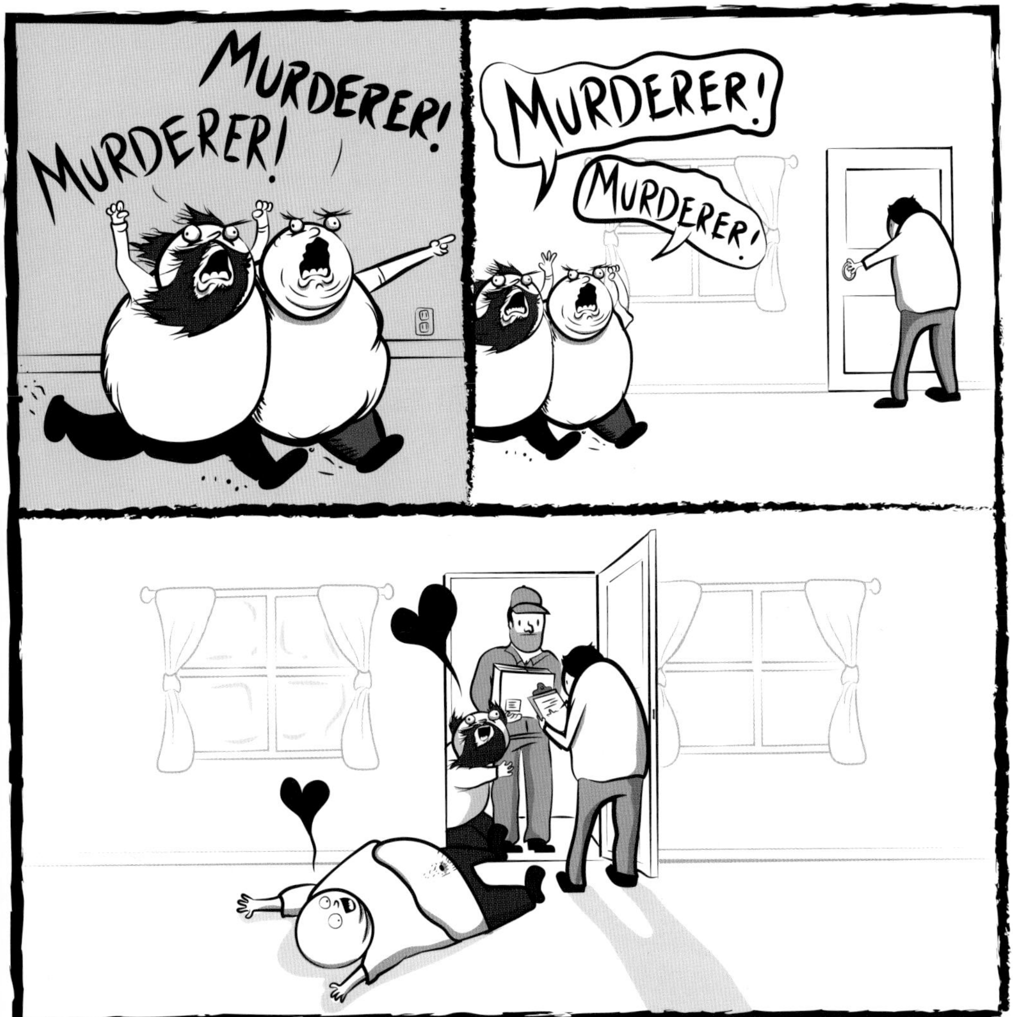
MURDERER!
MURDERER!
MURDERER!
MURDERER!

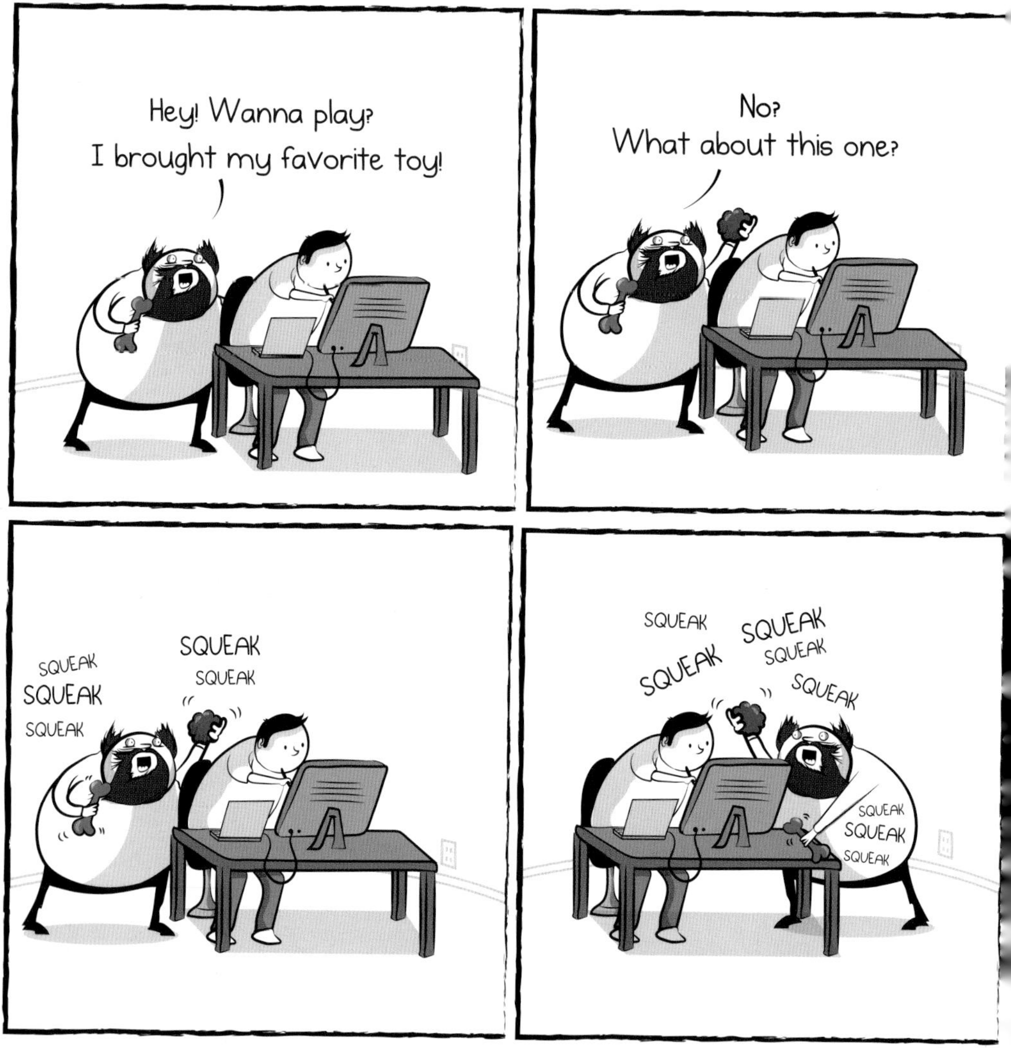
Hey! Wanna play?
I brought my favorite toy!
No?
What about this one?
SQUEAK
SQUEAK
SQUEAK
SQUEAK
SQUEAK
SQUEAK
SQUEAK
SQUEAK
SQUEAK
SQUEAK
SQUEAK
SQUEAK
SQUEAK

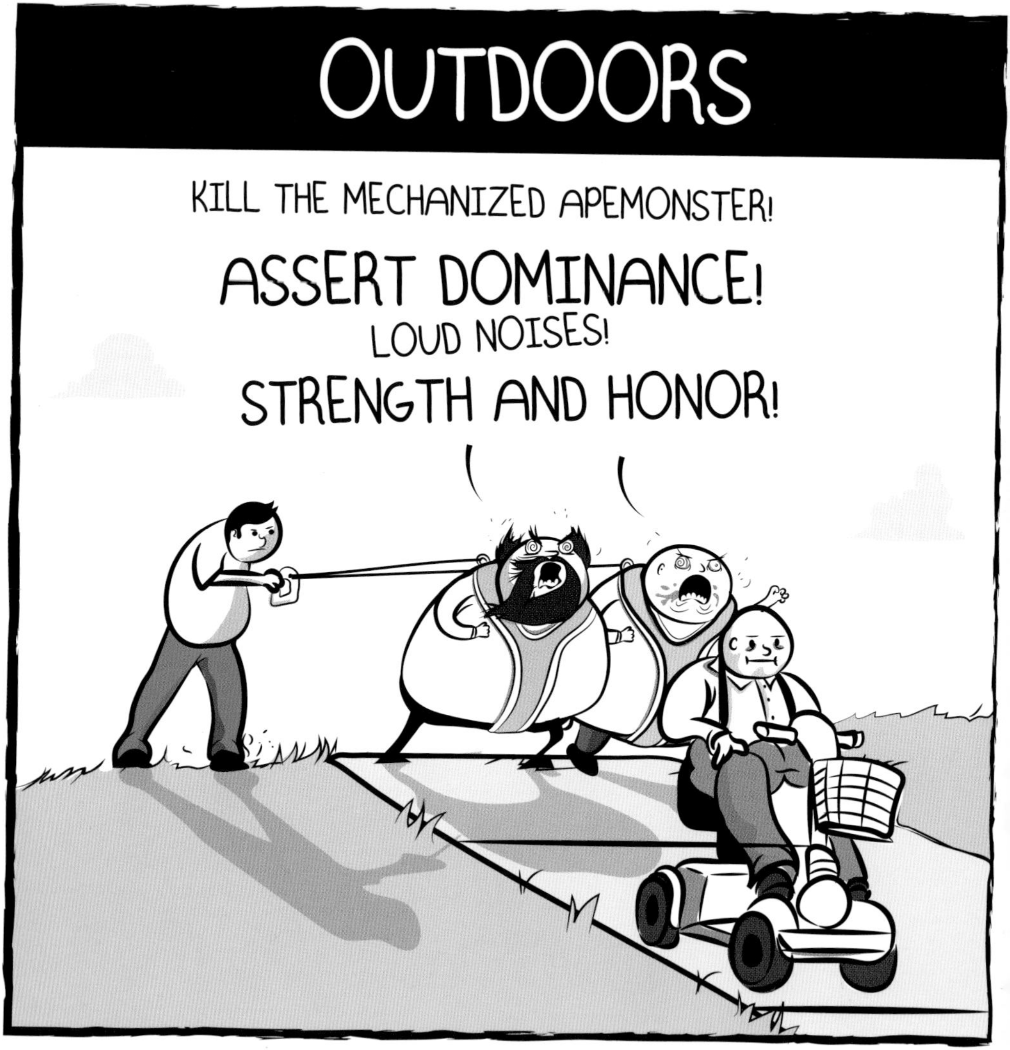
OUTDOORS
KILL THE MECHANIZED APEMONSTER!
ASSERT DOMINANCE!
LOUD NOISES!
STRENGTH AND HONOR!

INDOORS

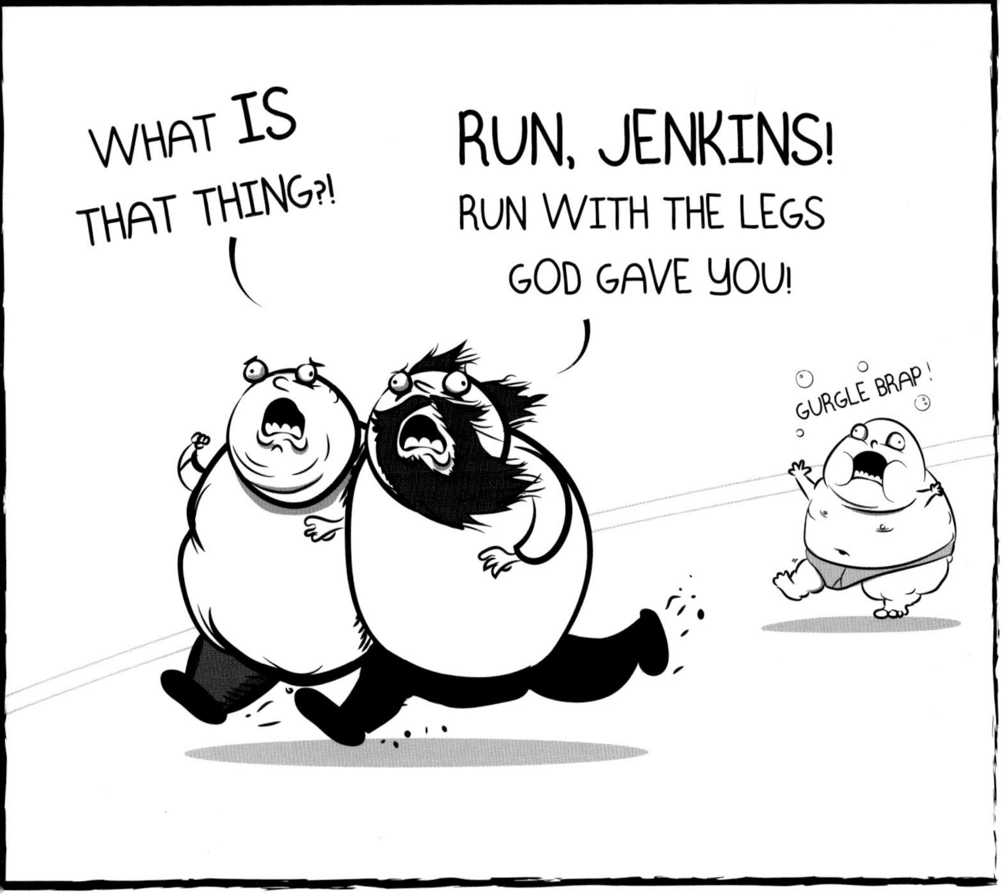
WHAT IS THAT THING?!
RUN, JENKINS! RUN WITH THE LEGS GOD GAVE YOU!
GURGLE BRAP!

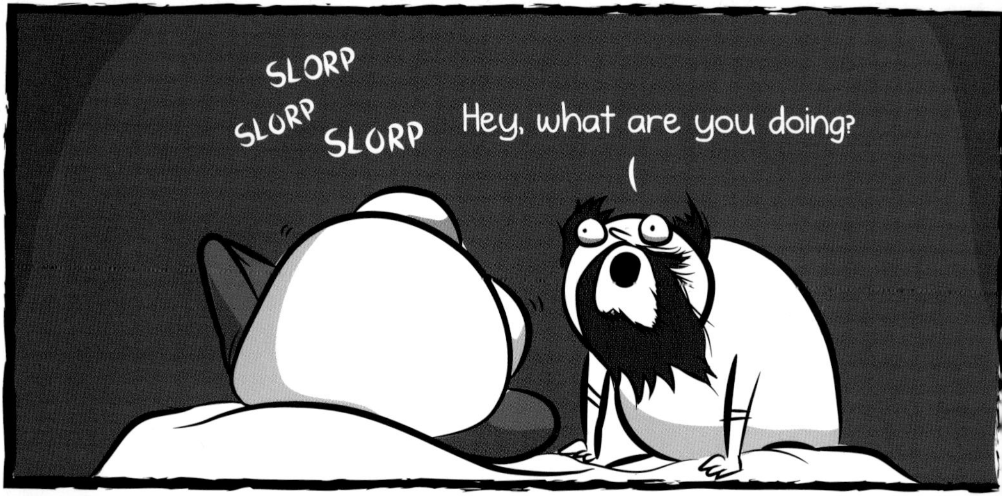
SLORP
SLORP
SLORP
Hey, what are you doing?

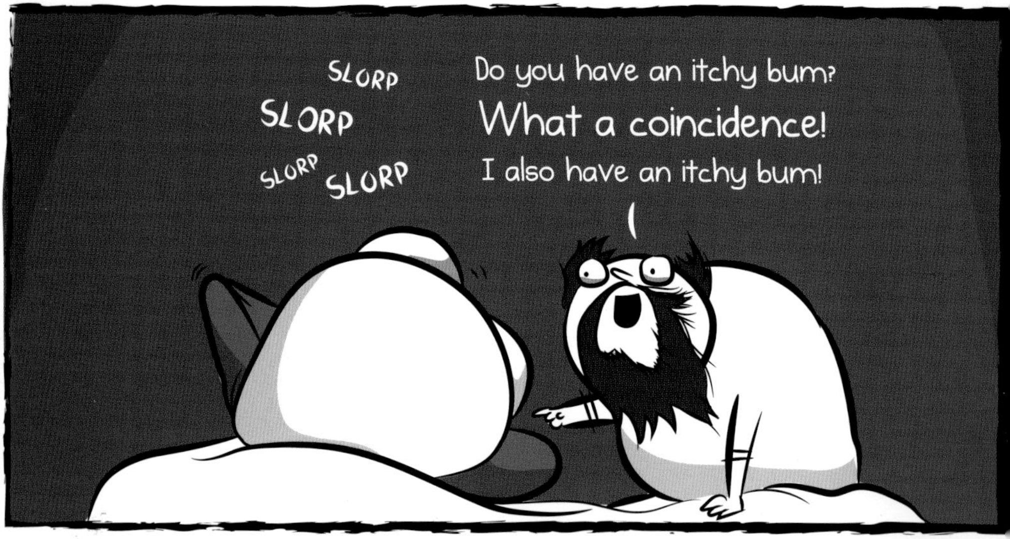
SLORP
SLORP
SLORP
SLORP
Do you have an itchy bum?
What a coincidence!
I also have an itchy bum!

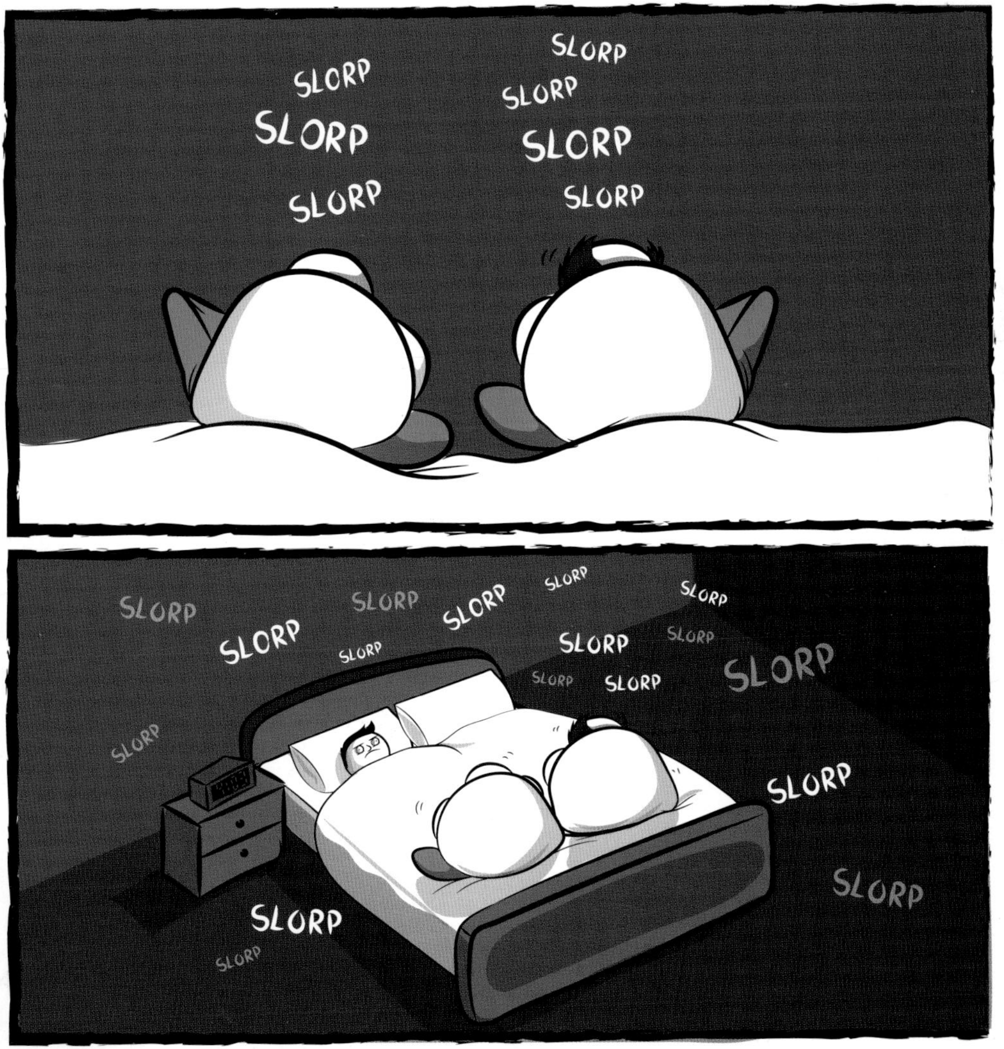
SLORP
SLORP
SLORP
SLORP
SLORP
SLORP
SLORP
SLORP
SLORP
SLORP
SLORP
SLORP
SLORP
SLORP
SLORP
SLORP
SLORP
SLORP
SLORP
SLORP
SLORP
SLORP
SLORP
SLORP

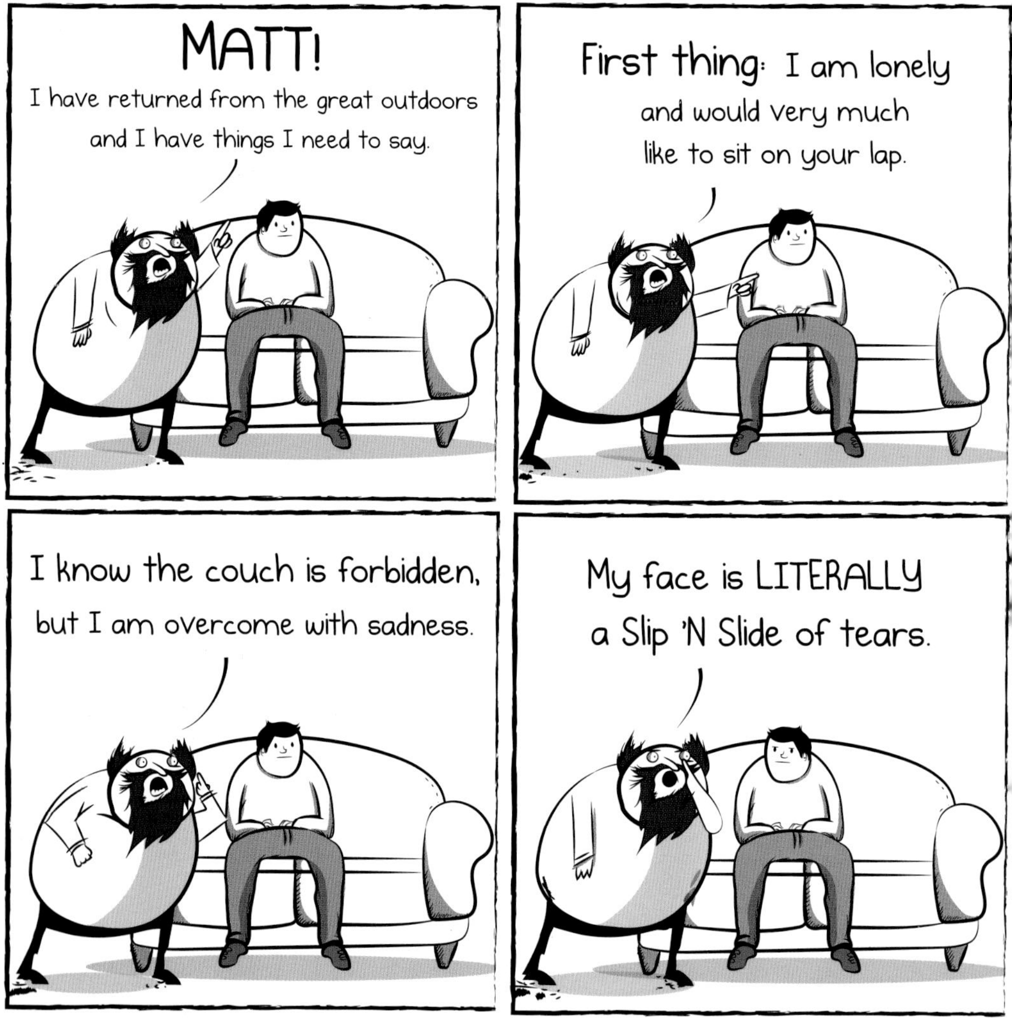
MATT!
I have returned from the great outdoors and I have things I need to say.
First thing: I am lonely and would very much like to sit on your lap.
I know the couch is forbidden, but I am overcome with sadness.
My face is LITERALLY a Slip 'N Slide of tears.

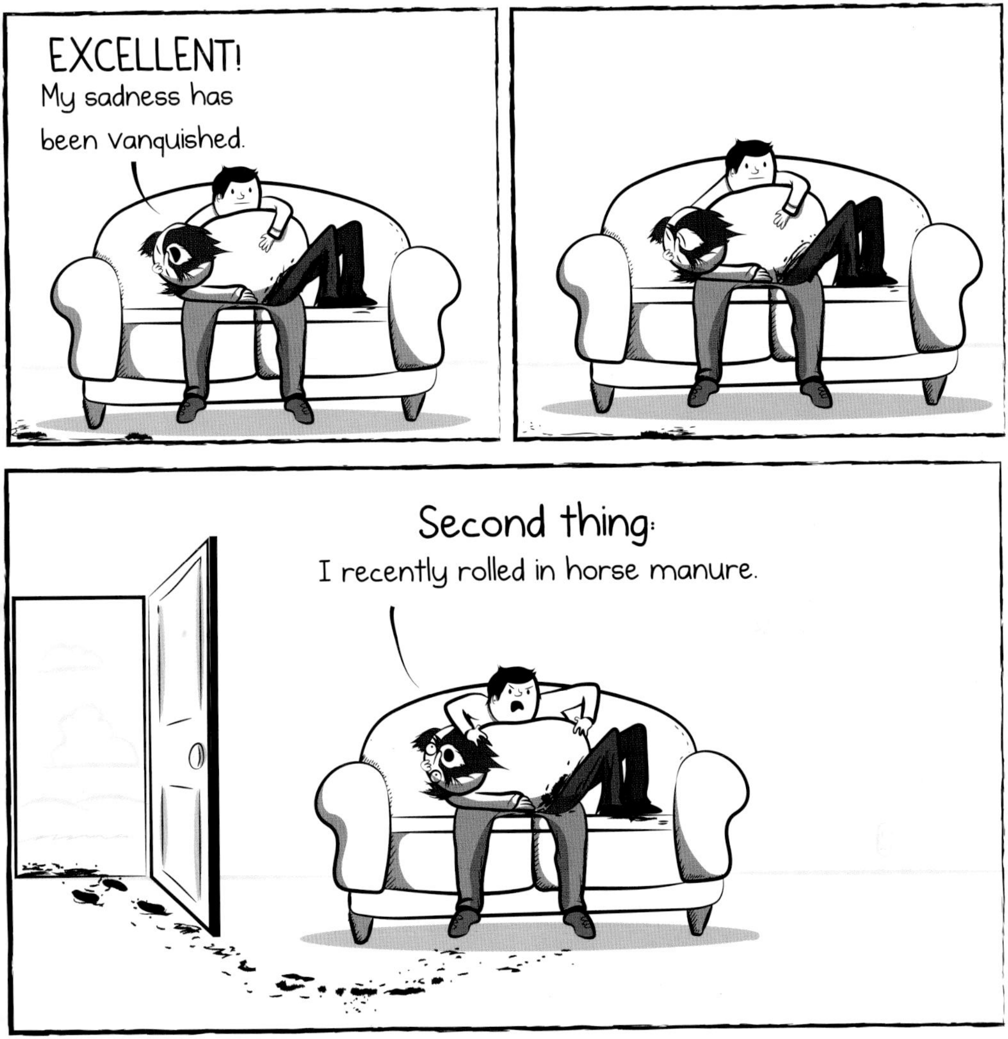
EXCELLENT!
My sadness has been vanquished.
Second thing:
I recently rolled in horse manure.

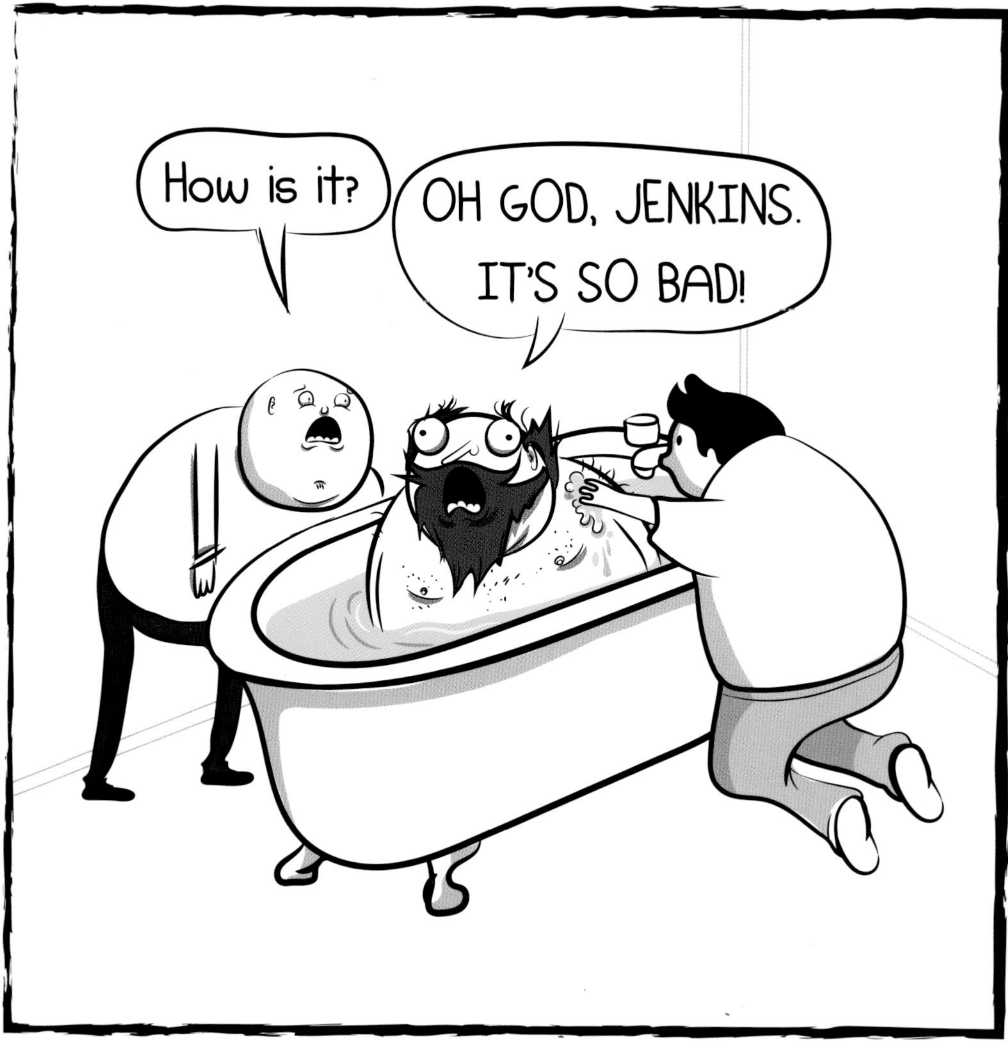
How is it?
OH GOD, JENKINS. IT'S SO BAD!

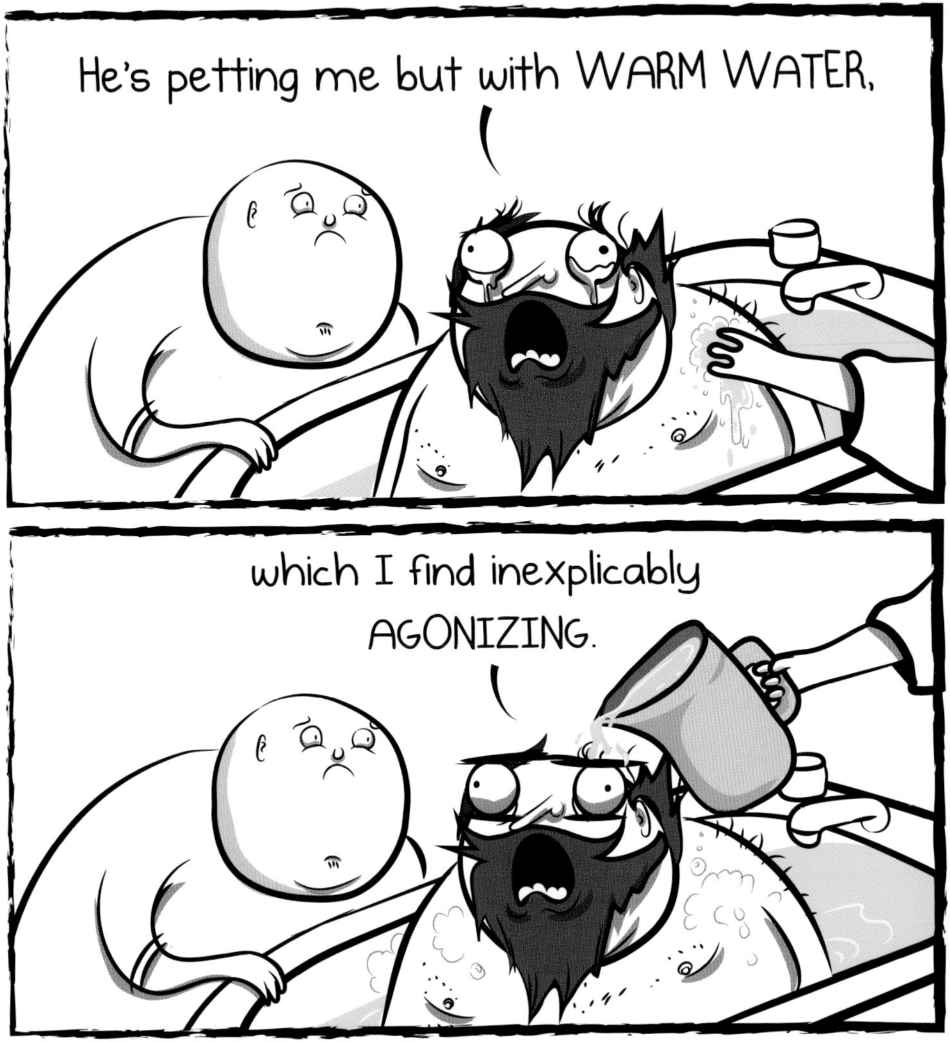
He's petting me but with WARM WATER,
which I find inexplicably
AGONIZING.

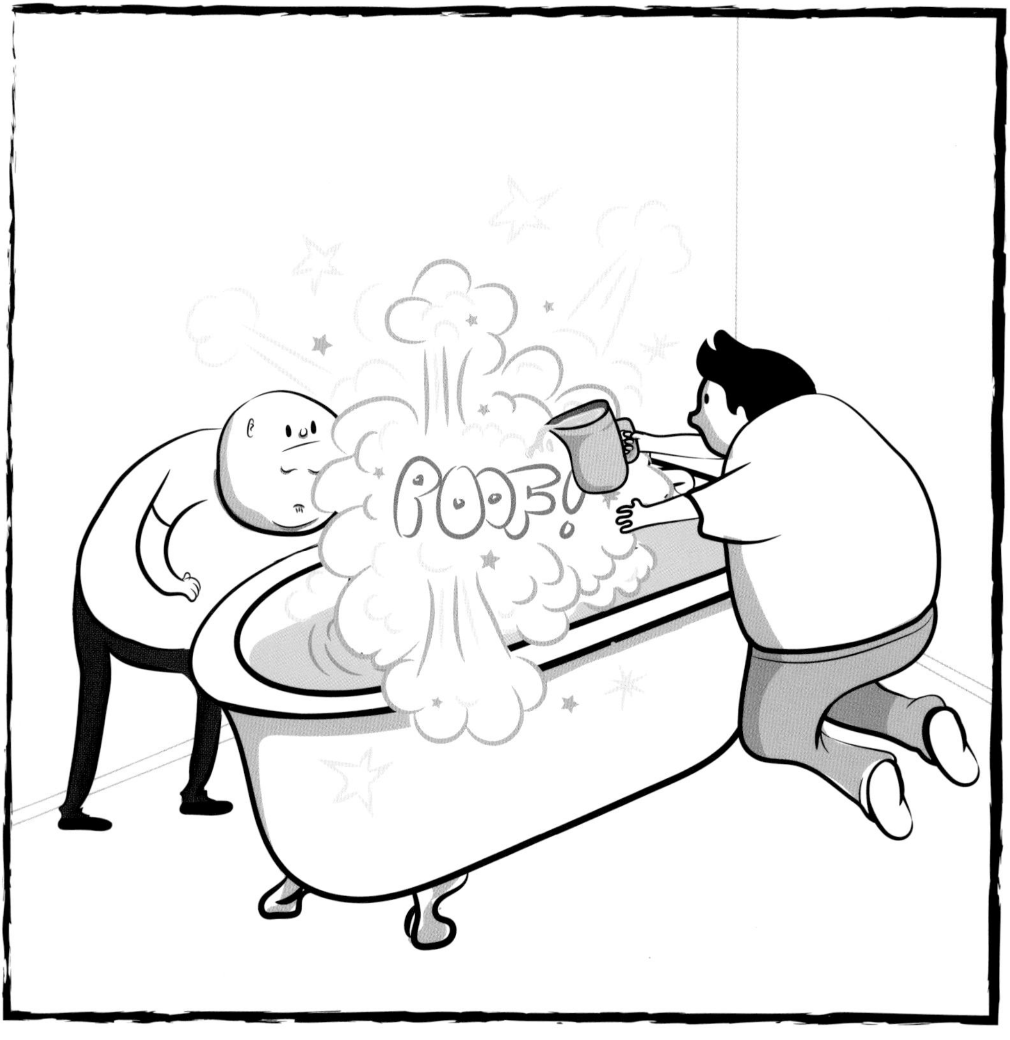
POOF!

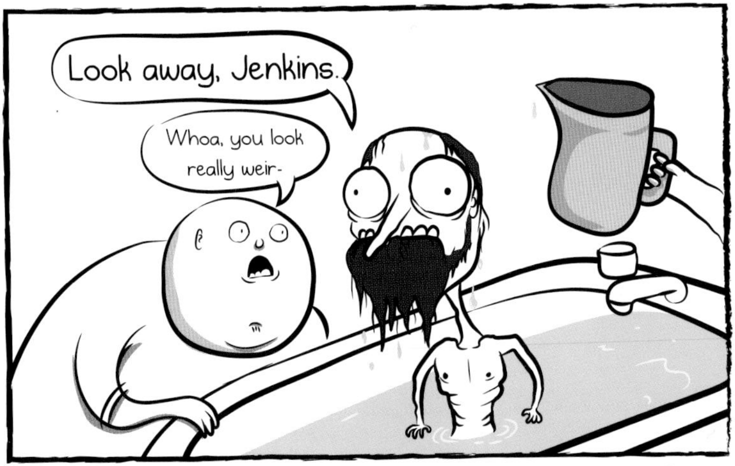
Look away, Jenkins.
Whoa, you look really weir-

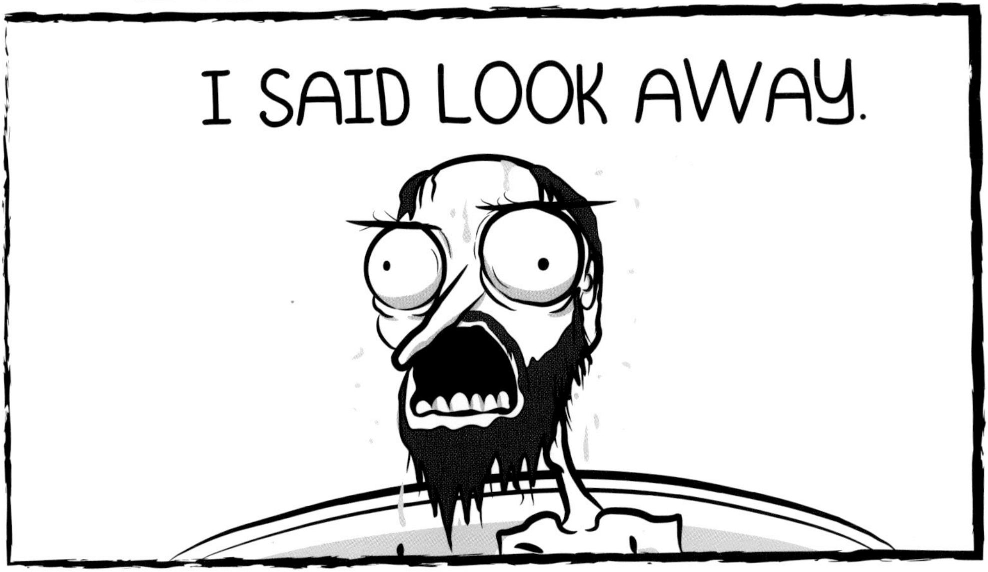
I SAID LOOK AWAY.

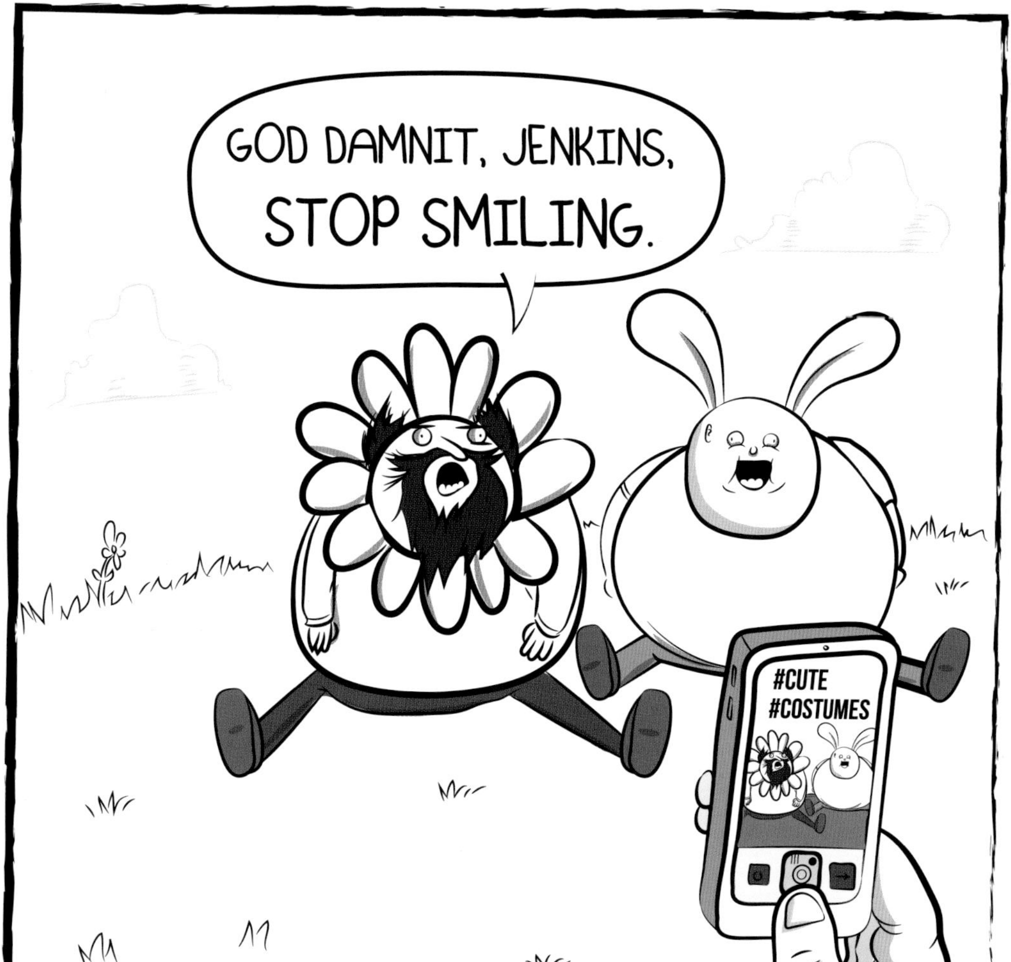
GOD DAMNIT, JENKINS, STOP SMILING.
#CUTE
#COSTUMES

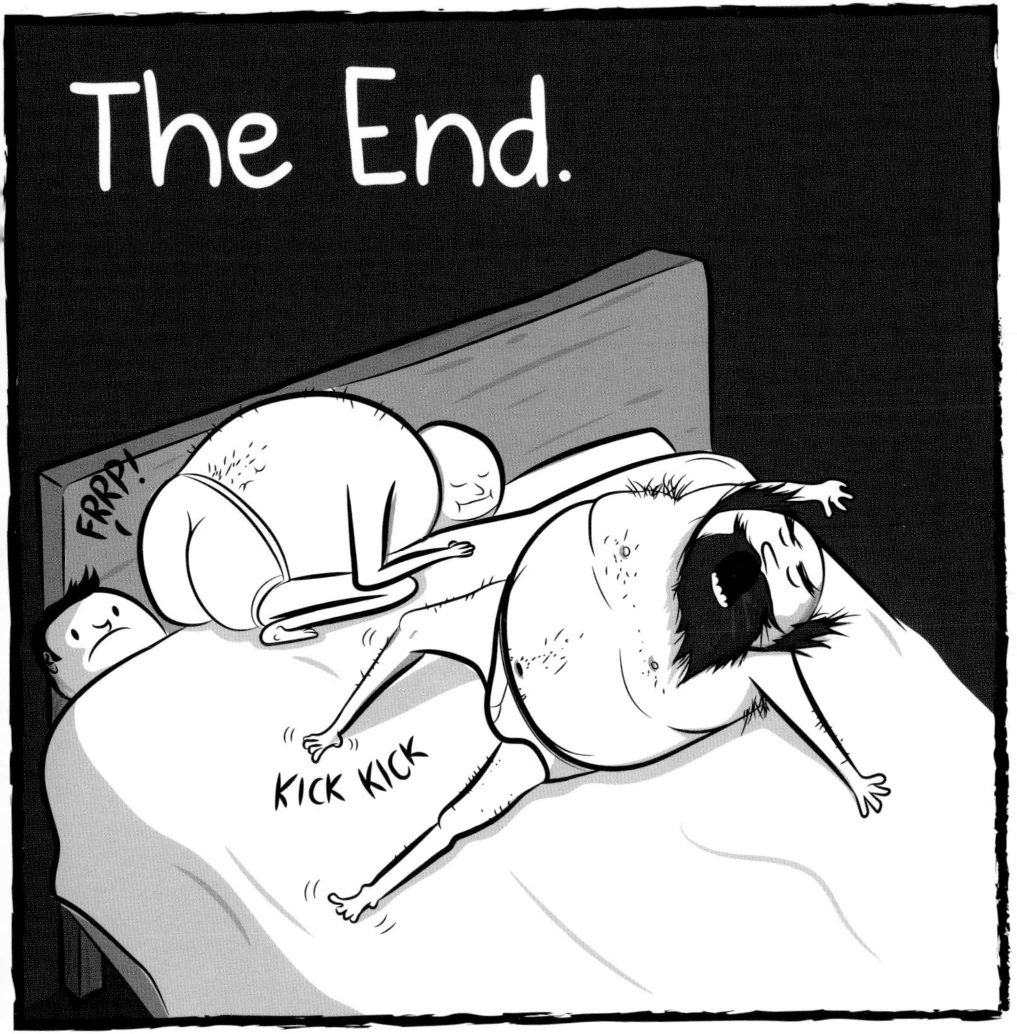
The End.
FRRP!
KICK KICK

About the author

This book was written and drawn by

Matthew Inman,

AKA The Oatmeal.

Matthew lives in Seattle, Washington, where he spends a lot of time cartooning in his underwear.

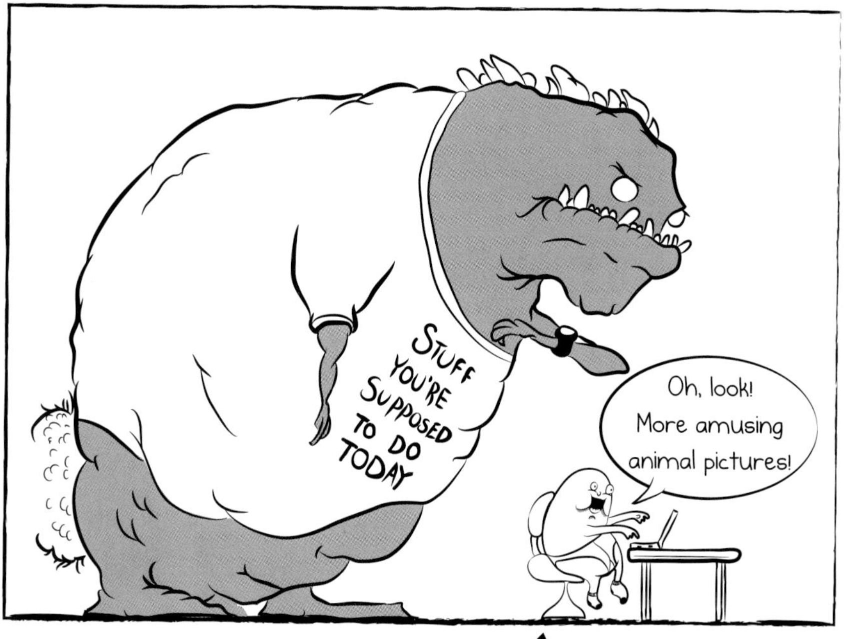
STUFF YOU'RE SUPPOSED TO DO TODAY
Oh, look! More amusing animal pictures!

↑3 p.m. Still in underpants.